A Leaf About To Fall
Selected Poems

İLHAN BERK, one of Turkey's most influential and innovative poets, was born in the Aegean city of Manisa. He is the award-winning author of more than two dozen books of poetry, as well as volumes of critical and biographical prose. He is also an acclaimed visual artist. Today Berk lives in the town of Bodrum.

GEORGE MESSO is a poet, translator, and editor. His books include *From the Pine Observatory* (2000), *Aradaki Ses* (*The In-Between Voice*, 2005), *Entrances* (2006), and *Avrupa'nın Küçük Tanrıları* (*The Little Gods of Europe*, forthcoming 2007). He is the editor of *Near East Review*.

A Leaf About To Fall

Selected Poems

İLHAN BERK
Translated by George Messo

S
SALT

CAMBRIDGE

PUBLISHED BY SALT PUBLISHING
PO Box 937, Great Wilbraham, Cambridge PDO CB1 5JX United Kingdom

First published 2006

Printed and bound in the United Kingdom by Lightning Source

Typeset in Swift 9.5/13

ISBN-13 978 1 84471 274 8 paperback
ISBN-10 1 84471 274 5 paperback

TB

1 3 5 7 9 8 6 4 2

Contents

Acknowledgements

Several translations first appeared in earlier drafts in *Absinthe*, *Dialogue of Nations through Poetry in Translation*, *Near East Review*, *Orient Express*, *Other Poetry* and *Shearsman*.

I am grateful to UNESCO for funding my stay at The Baltic Centre for Writers and Translators in Gotland, Sweden, where these translations began.

My deep thanks to Şenol Bezci for his painstaking review and correction of the final manuscript and for his many valuable suggestions.

Context and Counter-Current
Introducing İlhan Berk

İlhan Berk was born in 1918 in the Aegean city of Manisa. He once said "If a poem is written and goes out into the world, something in the world has changed." Berk has been changing the world of Turkish poetry for the best part of seven decades. His innovative poetics have marked him out as one of the vital modernizing forces in contemporary Turkish literature and earned him a reputation as a literary *enfant terrible*, poetry's "Third Man." Yet others deride his linguistic experimentalism as the work of a "French renegade." Few poets in Turkey today would dispute the significance of his work and at the tender age of 87, more productive than ever, Berk remains a force to be reckoned with.

İlhan Berk graduated from Necatibey Teacher Training College in Balikesir and, after two years as a primary school teacher in Espiye, Giresun, entered Gazi Institute of Education (now Gazi University) in Ankara, graduating from the department of French in 1944. From 1945 to 1955 he taught French at various secondary schools and colleges in Zonguldak, Samsun and Kırşehir. In 1956 he joined the publications department of the state owned Ziraat Bank as a translator, where he stayed until his retirement in 1969.

His first poems appeared as early as the 1930's in magazines like *Varlık* (Presence) and *Uyanış* (Awakening). His first book, *Guneşi Yakanların Selamı* (Greetings of the Sun Burners, 1935), published by the Manisa Community Centre, was strongly influenced by the poetry of Nazım Hikmet. Yet even by the 1930's Turkish poetry was barely out of the Ottoman court, cramped by convention and seemingly marooned in a netherland of post-symbolism. Hikmet, who had almost

single-handedly set about upturning the status quo, was by 1938 serv-
ing a prison sentence for treason, his books banned. Much of Hikmet's
revolutionary poetic credo, his belief that poetry should address the
social and political concerns of everyday folk in a language free of arti-
face and intellectual pretention, lived on into the following decade
in *Varlık*, a magazine to which Berk continued to contribute along-
side leading "First New" poets Melih Cevdet Anday, Oktay Rifat and
Orhan Veli Kanık. It was Kanık who nailed the *First New* movement's
controversial manifesto in his collection, *Garip* (Strange, 1941):

> The literary taste on which the new poetry will base itself is no
> longer the taste of a minority class . . . The question is not to make
> a defense of class interests, but merely to explore the people's tastes,
> to determine them, and to make them reign supreme over art . . . In
> order to rescue ourselves from the stifling effects of the literatures
> which have dictated and shaped our tastes and judgments for too
> many years, we must dump overboard everything that those litera-
> tures have taught us. We wish it were possible to dump even
> language itself . . .[1]

Berk's subsequent poems of this period, in *Istanbul* (1947), *Günaydın
Yeryüzü* (*Goodmorning Earth*, 1952), *Türkiye Şarkısı* (*Song of Turkey*, 1953)
and *Köroğlu* (1955, named after a sixteenth century folk hero and
wandering minstrel) relied heavily on early modernist strategies of the
First New. But Berk was seldom, if ever, ideologically driven. The ambi-
tious scope of his early books, their oracular, legend-telling quality, the
colloquial musical structures and rythmns prompted one critic to
dub him "the Turkish Walt Whitman." In 1953, however, two years
before the last and most accomplished of his "Whitman period" books,
Köroğlu, Berk made a sudden and decisive break. The publication of his
poem "Saint-Antoine's Pigeons" in the magazine *Yenilik* was to signal a

---

1 Quoted in Halman, T.S. "Introduction" in Just For The Hell of It: 111 Poems
  by Orhan Veli Kanık, Multilingual Foreign Language Press, Istanbul, 1997.

paradigm shift in Turkish poetry, as pervasive and fundamental as the *First New*, a movement which would later be known as the "Second New."

Both the *First New* and the *Second New* were responses to Turkey's volatile, reactionary social and policial landscape. Just as the War of Independence had dramatically transformed Turkey from a Sultane into a modern Republic, so too the *First New* had dragged Turkish poetry, somewhat belatedly, into the twentieth century. By the end of World War II, however, the reformist platform of the first Republican government was beginning to look hollow. The routine arrest and imprisonment of left-wing activists, writers and intellectuals defined the increasingly hostile and conservative political ethos. By the late 1940's the painfully slow rate of reforms lead to Turkey's first multi-party election, amid widespread feelings of disillusionment and betrayal, feelings which many on the politicial left were now wary to voice for fear of arrest. It's little wonder, then, that the *First New*'s naive, optimistic celebrations of everyday life seemed to many poets, including Berk, tragically out of place at a time when freedoms to speak on social issues were being so violently suppressed. With bitter irony it was the same incoming far-right nationalist government of Adnan Menderes which initiated Nazım Hikmet's release, following a general amnesty of political prisoners, a government which was to preside over one of the darkest and most politically repressive periods in the Republic's history. Indeed, it was Hikmet's fear of re-arrest that had him flee Turkey only six months after his release.

It was into such a climate, then, that Berk's now famous poem "Saint-Antoine's Pigeons" fell, with its fragmentation, its disruptive grammatical juxtapositions, its sexually suggestive and historically minded rhetoric, its radical and shocking disavowal of the *First New*'s "public language". What began with "Saint-Antoine's Pigeon's" was a poetry of the personal in which formerly pre-conceived notions such as self and identity, authority and history, language and freedom were now funadamentally questioned and challenged. In the Menderes climate of violent, psychotic political paranoia the *Second New* took nothing for granted, not even meaning itself, castigating the semantic demands on the poem in a poetry that made little sense as public address.

If the *First New* was an explosion the *Second New* was seen by many of Berk's contemporaries as a catastrophic implosion, a reckless and suicidal assault on the very idea of poetry itself. The poet, now distanced from society, was little more than a solipsist, babbling in a language only he could understand. Over the next three dacades Berk became a fierce and outspoken defender of his own new poetry and the new poetries of Ece Ayhan, Edip Cansever, Cemal Süreya and Turgut Uyar. Collectively, as the *Second New*, these poets revitalised Turkish literature, insisting, as they did, that poetry be no longer just a matter of social obligation and political commitment but a matter of personal survival, of our very existence.

"I have regarded the world" Berk once said "as a place to write in, not to live in." Today Berk lives in the Aegean town of Bodrum, known to antiquity as Halicarnassos. He is the author of more than two dozen books of poetry, as well as volumes of critical and biographical prose. He is also an acclaimed visual artist. He translated a selection of Ezra Pounds' *Cantos* in 1948 and a celebrated version of Arthur Rimbaud in 1962. His awards for poetry include The Turkish Language Association Poetry Prize for *Kül* (*Ash*, 1979), the Bahçet Necatigil Prize for İstanbul Kitabı (*Book of Istanbul*, 1980), the 1983 Yeditepe Poetry Award for *Deniz Eskisi—Şiirin Gizli Tarihi* (*In The Sea's Wake—The Secret History of Poetry*, 1982) and the Sedat Simavi Literature Prize for *Güzel Irmak* (*Beautiful River*, 1988). In 2002 Berk brought his poetic trilogy of *Ev*

(*House*), *Çok Yaşasın Sayılar* (*Long Live Numbers*) and *Birşey Olanlarla Birşey Olmayanlar* (*Those That Are And Those That Are Not*) together under the title *Şeyler Kitabı* (*The Book of Things*, 2002), a monumental project which he described as a need "to add dust, mud, rubbish, stone, dot, dash, question mark and slug" to his "reputation as a man of small subjects." Berk's writing has been a process of steady, careful refinement and, though his language has been ever-changing, the vision has remained remarkably clear. New poems continue to appear. "The important thing" Berk says "is to live the life of poetry, the writing always comes later."

George Messo

Evening with a Sprig of Sweet Basil

When she saw a sprig of sweet basil in the door
"Someone called" she said, "whoever could it be?"
She pulled a string, pushed open the door. Looked around.
Three more leaves fell from the vine. Three dry leaves.
She saw the pomegranate splitting, as if for the first time.
She left the onions and salt she carried in the kitchen.
"It's evening" she said, entering the room.
She went to change her clothes, put oil in the lamp.
Put wood in the stove, lit a flame. Noise
coming from her neighbours. Were they frying fish?
Then she sat with evening in her hand,
      that branch of sweet basil.

Poem for a Father Looking for His Lost Son

"How often", he said, "will this boy run away?
He ran away at twelve, at sixteen he's running now."
This is how he spoke, and then fell silent. Pushing
the long hairs of his moustache to the left side of his mouth.
Had he come from Erzurum, or from Tunceli?
For the first time he understood
                        how big the world now was,
then he closed up inside himself
                        watching the bird
hover and circle in the air.

We too fell silent,
                        each locked within ourselves.

Beautiful River

My little love, this is your voice, beautiful river
One kissed first by the wind and then by me
These unfinished poems are your ankles
Your breath, your scent, your belly, your shaded eyes
Your bare breasts, your full lips
Your large eyes like this till morning
Your slender form, your hair, your red mouth
Then this bed on which we made love
Then this, my time-worn old face
Your pubis, your filly neck, your infant hands
I look you up and down this way
Entangling our incredible hands and feet.

What a Woman Sees Each Night from a Coast

Every night she comes alone and sits on the coast.
Every night a large circular saw works away, shrieking.

A bulldozer takes up the road.

Children lorries horses cars
every night that's all she sees.

Apart from that, a desecrated spring, a swallow,
a tree, sometimes too a falling leaf.

And something called the sky
clinging to the corner of her mouth.

The Man Walking Along a Sunny Coast

Someone is walking along the sunny coast
holding his shadow in his hand, together. Empty
sky.
        In his hands tomatoes peppers cucumbers.
Women passing with their nets. Bees, seaweed,
the sea flat as a plain following on behind.

—They say, winter is around the corner. And quinces
grew early this year. They say, if quinces come early
winter will be long.
                He doesn't hear.
Holds his shadow tightly in his hand,
walks along the coast,
                beyond the wagging tongues.

Old Boatmen

Mornings
    they come to the same place and sit.
Stare at the sea. Their voices
as if they were voices from another world.

—Remember,
the boat was taking water. At the helm
we steered towards death and returned.

—A cormorant,
crashed down headfirst
into the helm and never came back up.

—That day my funeral flashed before my eyes
passing by
        on the shoulders of friends.

—Still in my ears
what Ateşoğlu said, We're sinking!

 All day they talk like this.
Stubbed out cigarrettes between their fingers.
Stare at the sea. Dead sea.
        Sky
comes and goes in the coffeehouse mirror
familiar faces from another time and place.

Visiting the Beloved Wife of a Dead Poet

'Papers, books' she said 'wherever I lay my hand.
A few half-finished poems, another somehow or other
complete. It was all there in the poems, wasn't it?
In one the sky grew pale, in others a street
came and went.
                    That was how we spent our lives.'

Her voice,
            as if coming from far away, faltered,
and then moved on in the quiet room. Then
she showed us a book that lay open on the desk
which the poet had touched, left for the last time.
'He sat there, reading this book,
and then we saw it slip from his hand.
That was all.'

            And that's what she said, her face
behind her hands, as if eclipsed
by the shadow of a passing cloud.

Season of the Hunt

Prologue

(O you! And O tea-time.) The house is woken. Halayik pours tea. The hand drops sugar into tea. Handfuls. Bedevi winds the clock. The Bey's slender bridge sways. *The castle gate creaks. One girl wakes another.*

> *. . . and the Bey leans forward and kisses you. The house gently sways and is gone.*
>
> *The child lets go of his paper boats. Returns, waits for tea.*
>
> +
>
> *The face sails far away.*

I

THE HUNT

The men go hunting. Hold birds in their hands. The women
are silent, waiting for the men. The men return with flowers. Swans
gaze at the men returning from the hunt. Fires burn. The women
sit, listening to a book being read. Birds and flowers listen too. A
peacock stands motionless, as if in a painting. A casement window
is opened from inside, closed from inside. Later a man comes and
teaches the women arithmetic. (In those days women knew arith-
metic.) A dog watches them, then leaves. Then the cavalrymen
come. No one thinks about the war. War is a kind of loneliness. It
enters not a single house. The girls have hands and feet. The Jew sits
before a bookrest, a girl comes in. One girl looks at the other girls.
The men are holding the women's hands. All the women's faces are
long,

> a long
> slender face
> enters painting.

In those days there are no Americans. Women wear underwear.
I begin a bawdy poem but can't finish it.

Later,
> women are in paintings. No one goes into houses. No one
goes out for the hunt. Though they do return. A book remains
always open. A window is closed to the sky,

(we see it all).

II

THE WOMEN

First it is the women who meet him. First a woman firms up her breasts, then all the women firm up their breasts.

The men fall alseep.

I used to play. I'd run my hand over the edge of his mouth. Two rowing boats slid into the sea. Then we'd sit and watch them. A woman washes herself beside us. I wash her too. I take her lines and leave. The woman holds you by the hips. She bangs against doors. Slender.

Outside they race a horse
                    pure white
                            and let it go.

+

Sometime later it returns.
Black.

III

THE RAMPART

(a)

Upstairs is loneliness. Rampart closes in on rampart. Closes in
on sheep, silk, Arabian red. The merchant puts down his silks and
leaves. Embroidery frames are stretced. The girls' slender faces take
form. A boy with a thousand locks of hair holds the rampart gate.
Musicians enter. They twist their moustaches for the Sultan.

The islands remain far away.

A piece of silk falls into the water. Three Beys laugh. We're
surprised.

(b)

The Queen descends,
                    ancient.
With her
                    something else
yellow
like love.

IV

THE CHILD

(The women were left downstairs.)
Grapes were harvested. A tall child
                   placed
                   his foot on ours.

(Trees, and water crossing water. The black servant fetches the mirror, the needlebox. The sheep's fleece is sheared and combed. A woman makes love to a balcony. Galleons arrive.)

From China.

She opens a book and reads. She glances from a window out through another. A black servant passes with a painting. Sleep leans against a balcony.

   +

The child goes always by a canal.

V

THE MEN

. . . and the men take whatever is there and join the fleet. Then
the Sultan comes in. (Suddenly I see your hands are different.) The
Sultan crosses his legs and sits down. Your own feet disappear.
Night disappears too.

Later, that tall
handsome
man
takes you. You.

The Sultan continues to sit. He stares. (A Copt leaves, caressing
the cord.) That man doesn't leave you. He laughs. The feet you
possess rest against my sky, feet that never were yours. The Sultan
leaves. The fleet pauses. Perhaps he never stands. The Sultan. Too
weak. And so as not to bore him the rope climbers, bridges, tents,
those who twirl dishes in the air never leave, and never stop.
Wherever can I take you? Wherever is there? Perhaps a blood-soaked severed
hand inside a carriage. Perhaps they're firing on the galley ships and castles
in our absence.

And the Sultan stands up. (The buses stop.)

VI

Upstairs a woman takes a woman's mouth in her mouth.

VII

FLOW

The baby is layed out. As if it had just been born. Some water is
released at first. Copious. Slippery. Slides towards other water. Then
it spreads out like a jellyfish, embraces the other water. The water
becames rough, and stays so. Then for some reason changes, as if
washed with soap.

Lifeless, it falls.

The girls pass by. The men avert their eyes. They too pass with-
out stopping. The yellow stain remains on the wooden floor and
won't come off.

+

I pick up one of the children and go.

VIII

ME

Downstairs they carry a white cross. The child Muhammed is
laughing out of the walls. Chora feeds the birds from on top of
her beautiful, black camel. Houses of three and four floors. Arched,
small, with neither windows nor walls. Yellow balconies. And white
beds. (In every epoch beds are white. In our time too they are white.)
There is much weeping. Winter sherbets are brought and rosewater
sprinkled. The donkeys and camels are awsome. An Arab gathers
the girls and strips them. The girls cover their breasts. In a picture
Zeus kidnaps Europa, then rapes her. (How beautifully the man
holds the book of stories. Angels came but didn't descend.)

And in secret rooms they make love. The women admit no one
and make love. Having grown, they move down to the bedroom.
Our white sides attract them. Perhaps it is your hands they love.

I am weak. I can't stand. I stare. I look and I am weak. I wear a
new crescent shirt. The horses wait at the gate, as always.

Having grown you go downstairs.
Having grown from my looking.

+

I leave.

IX

SEFINE

One night the hunting ends. Sefine comes out. The galleons come to a halt. Three Beys step off their horses. With them partridges, falcons, mountbanks. Cartridges, the whole fleet. (A man makes the corpse laugh.) The Queen takes a pheasant and leaves. Then men hand out the dead game. Boys light fires. And women leave a paper-light wind in their wake. The galley stops. Copper trays of halva come in. The dead game stinks. We leave the sky. Suddenly the house fills and then recedes. The tents come down. A man puts down the game. *What a beautiful child is the hunted animal. Its naked feet.*

I set the galley aflame. I'm there with the smell of fresh meat. The meat withdraws and waits. The copper pans and rice are still. Girls come for the birds. They cross over the canal. They hold their hands to the fire and keep them there.

You climb continously up and down a ladder.

The hunt rises.

X

Epilogue

(O you! And O. . .) The dead bring in the night. We look on. The black servant lights the lamp. Girls come out. The horse doesn't rear. The corpse grows pale. Sky enters. Rolls up carpets. Calls out to the girls. A hand closes the page. *Voices go downstairs. Wander around the house, come in, then make off with the water jug.*

It remains yellow. The nail cutter comes, clips the dead Sultan's fingernails and toenails.

The corpse is bored. Gives the carnation a shove.

Me, I go down a canal.

Paris, 1964

[18]

The History of a Face

I. History

We share with you the same history. The same suns,
the same winds. We pass through the same grape harvest.

The loneliness of a solitary stream
the voices of children playing in a schoolyard.

A morning's rise, its tides, its suddenness;
the endlessness and finality of a rose.

The same rain, the same flood, the same nomadic tribes of wind;
the sameness and indestructibility of dawn.

II. Voice

You are an underground stream
        in the mountain republic of Burgaz.
I am an ordinary writer
        in your republic's
abandonment, the one whose job it is to spread
the sparkle of windross, compasses, soundings and rainbows.

        So says a voice
deep within our ear,
as if from an old seaman
at the helm of a sunken boat.

When I stopped and looked at you
you were like coppiced trees, like meadows.
Sky swept past
and the eyes of Burgaz seamen were with that passing sky.

As for me, my ears were always pricked to that voice.

III. Exile

You are an island on an ancient map
from which an ancient people take water.

On your island I am the sun, alcohol and boredom.

You are the island's morning, its evening;
I am its night.

You are its waterways, trees, meadows and suns;
I am your nightmare.

You are the people's wheat, their pastures and streams;
I am their desolation.

You are the crowds through which I pass;
I am the exile of your isle.

Inscription on a Grave

"I, Ali Nalbantoğlu, born 1304,
                    from Istanköy.
Tallest of three brothers.

Nameless, untitled in this world,
and so too here.

                    My legacy?
I crawled my way to seventy-four
And now lay here, in Halikarnassos."

That's an inscription a friend and I
stopped to read at the end of a long lane
one late October
                    around noon.

Dead

I

ON THE FRONTIER OF PAIN

The dead write their names in capitals
on the wall of a room pocked with holes.

Casting its shadow full-length
with two letters.

Ears atune to the sound of water
because the blood is fresh

and it will leave its place
for the shore of an uprising.

II

DEATH

Has death changed its ways or what?
It scares itself

in self denial.
Its blood.

Its blood seeps out at terrific speed
and gathers.

Now the fire is slowly rising to its feet
because death has been arrested.

III

ABOUT TO LEAVE

The dead:
—Who darkened the sky like this?
They say: Ask this
of the poet!

On the frontier of pain
about to leave.

This is one of the questions that will be asked.

IV

Death was scrutinized.

As if Death were a Daily Routine

The road twists and turns. Eventually we stopped there.
We saw her through the open door,
                              sat spinning wool,
the spindle in her hand.
A large ball of wool had rolled and stopped at the door.
We stretched our heads around the threshold:
                              "How are you?" we asked.
As if changing the place of a chair
"We're dying, see!" She said
                              without raising her head.
As if death were a daily routine.

Wind was pounding the sea in front of her
which now and then she raised her head to see.

A Shoreside Coffeehouse

Day was underway. Had we ordered our sage teas?
Three people sat in a corner patching a net, some
playing dominoes, some of us lighting cigarette
after cigarette. As if the world had stopped,
absorbed in our own and each others thoughts.
Swallows were striking against the glass outside.
Suddenly a voice, his moustache-rumpled-face
—The sea's gone calm, he said. His eyes,
journeying across the sea, caught us all.
At the end of a long pause
he stood up.
    It was then we saw him
and the calmed sea.
    At that point we came out of ourselves.

Outside the sky was like a slice of bread.

The Men

The old coffeeseller straightens up the stools. The sky
is old. The coffeehouse empty. Olives, chickens, figs.
(On the floor a lime bucket, corn cobs, a water jug.)
This, just a fragment of the scene.

Later the men arrived.
Moustaches, full-grown beards. They opened sackcloths.
Ordered tea.
"Watch out for the pier, I said, that's all!"
One of them said, partly in anger, partly in rage.
"I said the same too" the tallest of them said.
The third, taciturn, listened with his head down.
His face like the front of a darkened door.

As we watched them talk
each of their moustaches dipped into their tea.
Then they were suddenly quiet
as if talking about someone who had recently died.
And before the sun went down they left.

Book of the Dead

I. On the Painful Death of a Discoverer

1.

In the beginning
all day he watched seabirds.

2.

He played dominoes for a year.
Found fault with his friends.

Had his photo taken with night.

3.

His face was a magnet for sun.
(He took only an afternoon snooze.)

4.

For five years in Anatolia's oldest history
he sold herring, salt and milk.
He drank raki, swept shop floors.

Then he discovered Troy.

5.

He died out walking with a panther.
(They say he dyed his beard red.)

II. Conversations On the Life of an Exalted Person, According to Ibn-i Hacer Heytemi

1.

—My father's clothes were neat.

He used excessive scents.

Like Henry IV you could recognise him by his smell before he
was seen.

2.

—"His name is remembered with that of a predatory bird."

He chewed frankincense gum to fend off forgetfulness.

3.

—We stayed with him for one year.

He never once took a rest.

4.

—He never sat in the shade of his creditor's trees.

Words dissolved like candy in his mouth.

5.

—Summers he worked in the silk trade.

He gave all of his profit away.

I swear not one of his race were slaves.

6.

—He never had a concubine

And cried before he prayed.

7.

—One day he saw a soldier eating meat

And asked how long the fish had lived.

An Old Salt

"The weather's turned, it's Lodos behind this," they say.
They set their eyes on the boats at sea.
They read the winds as if from a book
                    of a thousand pages.

"Lodos is a bitch, slippery, my father would say,
and he'd not measure any wind with that,"
said an old sea salt,
                    his face like a wall.

They look as if they haven't heard. As if
their days at sea were spent with cunning Odysseus.
Then, as if taking a sign
                    from the sky's changing form
they rise and go.
          The old salt stays. Eyes pegged to the sea.

The Women

They stop by the habour wall and are talking.
Their voices stir birds into flight; leaves are falling.
Who knows to which age these women belong.

You know, it's as if sometimes the world stops,
one day we were together pressing flowers
into a notebook:
        they're like that, women,
who knows when, or where, all at once
a voice from our past
        is right beside us.

The Sea Book

I

CHAWS

I read, stretched out, looked at the sail fish.
All day I kept saying this line to myself.
The weather was cloudy, it's cloudy I said.
I went out, walked around, checked on repairs.
I pulled a long face at the workers. A stone had fallen,
a plank out of place: I put them right. A child
dashed an octopus against pebbles. I smiled at the child
then I went and turned on a closed fountain.
A woman asked for a street and I showed the way.
Suddenly I recalled I was going swimming that evening
so I went to change. I saw day creeping away.
I sat down then and worked at my Sea Book.

II

A whole long day I watched the sea. Great sea.
Storms gathered in. I sat and chiselled out

a skiff. A road lapped its way to the sea,
later going down behind Pazardağ. Barely seen.

A Greek ship off shore was slowing, putting achor down.
Aganta! I shouted suddenly. The sea echoed back.

The city was water. Water everywhere. Water, water, water.
I threw a fish into the air and the skiff bowed under me.

—The day's shortened, air sharp as a knife! I said.
Then I got up and headed off for Threewells Street.

III

THE CITY

Today I rose early. I woke up the sea.
A man was holding up a squid, showing it off.
I leaned over to look in his eyes, they were skyblue, round.
He breathed deeply like a heavy labourer.
Three men sat drinking tea and reading the sky.
One was describing the Lodos wind, acting out
the part. "In Bodrum, before Christ, there were only
the Salmakis and Zephyria districts," said another.
I was thinking of the Dorians and Alexander the Great,
of Saint Peter's chateau and the chevalier de Naillac.
At six the sun came up and we all dispersed.

IV

HAY

I was on the coast, I suddenly remembered this today.
I climbed up and looked at the city from a hill.

A ruined monastery remained ruined,
I thought of its monks, a little of their women too.

I bent down and smelled a stem of hay, followed by
the long braying of a donkey, a goat melody. I was enraptured.

A man was painting a rusted boat.
I cast him my "hello" into the boat.

Then off I went to draw a sketch of a chimney.
Looking at myself in the evening light: hay from head to toe.

V

THOSE FROM KARYA

Who are those folk from Karya? Three times I asked. Then
I thought back to yesterday, how I'd been swimming.
I'd seen seaweed. I've wanted to write about it for years
and the sea's depths. Saying this I climbed into bed.
I've a terrible love of my body, my nose, my arms,
my feet; your hairs, my hairs as they rise
on my stomach; my eyelashes and your mouth.
Then my nakedness, my terrible nakedness,
my legs, my groin. That's why I stretch out
my body, why I grow the hairs in my ears.
For my body I say these things. Then? Then
—Who are those Karya folk? I ask, and fill my pipe.

VI

ECOLOGY

I'm learning to name plants. Grasses, flowers.
I take up a laurel. This is wormwood I say.

I'm beginning to inspect from several angles
I tear off a wormwood leaf, then its juice

seeps into my hand. I twist off a branch
from its stem. I count the rings

of a long thin willow branch, then place it
in a stream, alert to the world's opulent greens.

So it is, the whole day I strole around
then suddenly take up the pen to write.

For Homer

I

Homer lived a quiet life. Like mountain roads.
And quietly he prepared—like
water ready to flow—
for the foundations of poetry.

Like all the world's great poets
he studied bird and beast, the ferocious sea,
the days' first flames, the first waves.

This is why Homer alone resembles Homer.

II

We know Homer as the master of long poems
and long suffering.

So it was on earth
his long cloak and long frame departed and returned.

Reading Li Po

In the first dynasty the unit of measure for wheat, cloth, tools,
and gold was the sheep:

	40gr. wheat
	20 metres cloth
1 sheep:	2 axes
	3gr. gold

Then gold took the place of wheat, cloth, tools,
                                    the first time round, that is.
And: "The first paper money was seen in China," says Li Po, the
greatest of China's poets.

The first shock.

That day, slowly but surely, he left his beard to grow.

Sofia

In Alexander Nevski church a woman strolls with her kids
as though in a garden. Two men are praying.

Standing like a black candle a priest stares at me
his face the colour of lemon, his slender hands yellow.

I walk, hands in pockets. Voices from Ruski Boulevard—
is it a woman calling from window to window?

Or a rose, I wonder, falling into morning?
I set my watch to the time of a Bulgarian peasant

his name begins with G, but he can't pronounce G
so I stop a streetseller and ask the way to a long street

because a woman is arranging flowers
I understand why her hands are thin and her face white.

One late afternoon I look for Dobruja Street in Sophia
with Hussein. He chews his whiskers constantly.

View

Unmoving sea. Empty sky. Near oleanders
the old boatman pulls his boat ashore and repairs it.
Bees, and housemartins turn above his head.
Not a sound. With his saw, nails and birds
every morning he finds himself part of the scene.
After a while the sea's skin, which we know, moves,
later checkers are pushed in the teahouse.
Then men women and children begin to pass
with water jugs and bundles in their hands.
It's then, at that moment, they stop and wave to him.
Weren't they also part of the scene?

Hamam Street

Returning, sunlight filled the street,
sunlight on your face.
           The road,
was it twisting? We saw the women.
Sky, as if it were their embroidery,
with flocks of birds they'd brought down,
                         ashen.

They went to put oil in the lamps, then
gathered up their needlework, their birds,
             from the life of the street.

We were sick with love,
             do you remember?
From behind us a flock of swallows took flight.

In the Sea's Wake

We were walking. Were we walking? Sun went down.
You beat around like sea against the coast.

A boy
barged past, in the corner of his mouth
a stem of grass.

That faded day in 1979
your mouth was two green leaves
and I was there in your mouth's rose.

(A woman on the Council Estate
opened and closed her windows,
readied, with time for evening.)

Novembers

Have you ever seen a city razed to the ground?
So what if I have? Whenever and where it was

stays with me, my acrid history.

Know this

What is time
a November leaf
a child's vacilating mouth
a rose
a left-over, half-drunk glass of water.

Right over there in Topağacı I have my own rose-seller
his face like a closed shop in November,
like the oldest winds.

Me, I'm like a stopped clock in a far-off station
wind flocks around inside.

Know this.

A Street Leads Down to the Sea

I

Belgrade, like an old face on the wall. I'm looking
at Belgrade on the wall.

Men are climbing a rampart
a sailboat goes by.

Five thousand years earlier I'm dissembarking
with the Celts, our Celts. A Celtic soup,

saltless and oiley. Celt. Long whiskered,
blonde, blue-eyed.

Celt. From the mountains
and with a thousand-page book like the Bible.

II

Mihaila.
I'm walking through Mihaila.

Three girls pass by a street,
in the air three question marks remain.

In Gajava a woman lights two candles
I change the candles' place.

III

Sabrona Crekva. Jesus, dark and dejected.
I seize his open hands.

A street leads down to the sea—
is there a Serbian night in the street?

Three men are going up 29 November Street: me,
I'm tramping down Zeleni Venac with my three day beard.

Arma Viriumque Cano
(Vergilius)

I. SATURDAY DARKNESS

We will walk a thousand years
first we will enter a street

a Genoese will bring me news of you
I will wait for you naked

they see us from Hagia Sophia
there is no one who does not see

Saturday darkness
stares at the Polish church

we waited for a thousand years
we are together first in a poem.

Discarding their cloths to the night
they will run to the Sultan with news of us.

I can't say I will ever see you again
and we never see each other again.

II. RAMPARTS

You descend from royalty.
Me, I know nothing of empires.
One day we'll see, we're in the bazaar
there's Constantine VI, Saint Leo's hand,
     Jesus' sandals, that something-face in the bazaar
the Goth's obelisk and Balikli Monastery's suns
     there before the houses.
Istanbul had not yet fallen, what wonderful fish they fried
Istanbul just wouldn't fall.

We withdraw all the money minted in our name
     and won't mint more.
We take neither Beato Majano's nor Paolo Belini's medallions,
     we return them all.
Ramparts are of no use to us, nobody needs ramparts
Look, it's true, no one needs such things.
Your people built more than enough ramparts
and we've had more than enough grief.

Istanbul will never see me again.

III. LITTLE

One morning we woke and found all the gates locked and all the
    streets held.
We didn't take this easily.
Now I suppose the streets will no longer stop and start
    somewhere without you.
Without you a window won't open and the sea come to a halt
    before your house,
nor the rain suddenly think of pouring.
I don't know where you'd go if you go.
Maybe it's good in Byzantium, maybe bad, or maybe I can't tell.
I don't like streets without small shops and cafes, nor do I like
    the rooms and walls.
I can't stand kings.
Let's say what you said is true, let's say you were first into the
    street,
No barbeques, no frying fish.
You're in a street,
all the things I said were absent, green lettuce, quinces, the
    warmth of destitution,
a heap of things that never come to man on a day that will
    never come,
so there you are in such a place
Constantine VI has bequeathed all waters to you.
This does not change the universe.
This is not it.

IV. MAP OF THE FIRMAMENT

One night we are in the vast blackness of the sky.
At night, gazing at the entire sky
Saint Paul stroles around in his underwear
Constantine thinks only of the world
and here Leo II is more lonely than ever.
A galleon moves slowly past,
water is everywhere, at a standstill.
There is nothing at all in the sky,
a pity so many men are bored.

One day you and I see this together
One day you are not there, that day there is nothing.

V. The Gate of Ahmet I

Overwhelming convoys of fires, slaughters, deaths and tyrannies.
In such a night you call out to me.
Enough, you say, of this wrack and ruin, this enmity,
       let them end at the gate of Ahmet I and rear their heads no
more.
Let us not know murder.
Take one step and an unending unscrinkable chasm opens before
us.
Fires solve nothing, massacres put nothing right.
Look how far I am from you yet nothing is changed.
Our waking one morning spoils nothing, puts nothing on track.
Only love plucks me from my place, carries me to unknown parts.
We travelled long and so we came to our end.

At the gate of Ahmet II
ground was taken again.

VI. Invitation

Don't call for me I can see you.
I'll put out these fires and come.

The Grieving Stream

Each morning my job it was
to take this plain from you
and raise it.

Each morning
my loveliest task in this world
was to magnify
              and beautify life.

There Have Been Trees I Have Made Friends With

"I filled silence with names." Codified things. I have known the sky's and the trees' infancy. There have been trees I have made friends with. There still are. I didn't understand the Milky Way. Nor numbers. (They behaved as if they had yet to be discovered.) Except for eight (5+3) with whom I became intimate friends. (Who hasn't?) A little with zero too. (It's not been so easy to find zero.) I've heard terrible things about three. Why? I don't know. To know is a number. And I've also met one. You can't think with one. Some numbers are born guilty. One of them is one. I loved stones without asking why. The relation between the pebble's name and its shape has not been proved. I couldn't find a thing on the history of black amber. Fine. Mystery is everything. There are some consonants I couldn't read. (The letter's spirit abounds in consonants. American Indians knew this well.) I accompanied birds. Except for the turtle-dove, birds know nothing of numbers. Horses, I understood, don't dream in the East. (In Homer horses weep.) I have seen mountains while walking. And thinking as they walked. Recognition impedes reason. *The World is ours!* Said the snails, talking among themselves. I can't say I understand that. Nor that I don't understand it. One should read snails.

As you talk about rivers the rivers themselves are talking, grasses are in their eyes. Time is an illusion. Write this down somewhere. It's not true that spirit has no outward facing view. Jesus' ghost still roams the earth. (I only ask. It's only to question that one writes.) Those who forget their youth stagger in the morning. The rose exists because it is named. Stone got its name when its face was found. (Which is why masons turn stones around and around in their hands.)

I want to return to your eyes. And then . . . There's no such thing as "then." "Then" is outside history.

The Flower's Indescribable Grief: Yellow Crocus

We came first into the world
and as we did
we learnt to try to love.
Little did we know
we'd one day learn to mourn.

Tree

(To Eluard)

If this sky, brought suddenly to mind, decided to grow a little more
this desperate tree
would be erased.

Yesterday I Wasn't at Home, I Took to the Hills

The sun fathers a cloud in my pocket. I wrote: the stone is blind. Death has no future. Things have only names. And: "A name is a home." (Who was it said that?) Yesterday I wasn't at home, I took to the hills. A gorge looked at us, what it said still lingers in my mind. It was this: we sensed infinity within it. Objects are held in time. The tailors' lamplighter Hermusul Heramise's goatskin rose to its feet every spring. Rain cannot not rain. Stone, not fall.

What was I saying, the world has no thoughts. Grasses don't get bored. A pencil thinks it is a tree. The horizon, a hoopoe. I don't know about you, the world is here to be mythologized. It has, therefore, no other end. Transforming into a myth, to be a myth! That's what we call eternity.

Wherever I start, that's where I return. So I'm going. I have work to do on that grand statement, death.

Kizilirmak

7 October 1951
was a cold, dark, deserted night
we were thirty people, a knife wouldn't part our lips
then we saw you from the wagon
languorously flowing
we all took out our cigarettes, lit up
and sang folk songs.

A Forest in the South

If wheat grows now in Turkey
it grows, I swear, with love.
I swear lavander, opium poppies and thyme grow, with love.
Sheep, goats, cattle
corn, rice and oats
are grown and raised in this world with love.
For thousands of years rivers run down to see the world,
so we learn for thousands of years there are rivers flowing and
plants
    growing in the world's many and various parts
I talked with moss, ferns and fish
there's none that hasn't seen the world.

Now in the south if clover grows
like me it grows for a better life.
Poppies grow for this too, side by side with my roots.
If cotton opens whiter than before
its reason is the same.
I'm raised, thinking of every forest.
They too grow up thinking of all the forests,
like me, the whole of Turkey's forests.
We have reached such a point in the world's age
when no one loves the world better than anyone else,
I love the forests, rivers and hill pastures of England
    as much as life,
I love those of America no less.
Here water-logged rice fields, cotton and tobacco love each other
       no less.
Now garlic, grapevines and beans grow by embracing each other.
Now the steppes and mountains love loneliness no more,
now no one in the world loves loneliness.
Now in Iran and in Egypt and in Sudan they know why forests grow.
Now they know why viens of petrol flow
Now they know why everything in this world has life.

Towards Evening

I undressed   your voice
            said
towards evening your voice is sky

Fern

My name   is fern
        in the mouths
                of rivers

Garden

Stroling in the garden
grass apparently

            saw

                    you

Water Days I

Water

is looking for you,
comes even
to your feet.

Water Days II

I

was water long ago,
Thales
is my source.

Water Days III

The pebble

thinks
you
are water.

Water Days IV

A praying mantis
a hill
come and go

on the water's surface.

Water Days V

At the city gate
stands a puddle
as if
not of this world.

Water Days VI

      I

             am water

leave me

      let me run.

Death is Like Nothing Else

A waterlily leaf
swims
on the water's face:

Death is like nothing else.

Leaf

Leaf

doesn't know its shade
until

it falls to you.

Shadow Falls Across the Courtyard

Between the marshmallows
a tortoise
sticks out its head to see:

its shadow falls across the courtyard.

Stopping

You stopped

silence
stripped
you.

Goat Track

I'm a goat track
wending to you

just as
e
v
e
n
i
n
g

a
p
p
r
o
a
c
h
e
s

As I Write

As I write
the paper
hears

you.

Ashes and End

Farewell
sky
fare-

well.

What the Tree Says

Leave me alone
says a tree
okay okay

I'll talk.

Trees

Trees
ask,
brothers

who exactly are we?

Words II

You suppose

they tell   of rivers
when words

talk of you.

Blonde-Haired Child

An open gas tap inscribes your name

I look you over with my mouth
I find you stuffed into oversized telephone books
I descend to your postage-stamp eyes
How a leaf
Noisily
Falls

That's how

        I love you
        Blonde-haired child.

Black Amber

One should start with your mouth when describing you.
My child, your mouth is Chinese silk, fires, black amber

Your mouth is a cold-water spring, a general strike
A foolish sea throwing itself from place to place

Your mouth is the boy selling dark blue birds in the market
It's a three-monthly magazine called *Field*

Our small rivers are your mouth
Coming down a narrow street each day into a small square

Your mouth is time in Bursa, covered bazaars
The night written in ancient letters

Your mouth is children, birds and summer days
Your mouth is the feel of silk in my mind.

Saint-Antoine's Pigeons

I. ELENI'S HANDS

One day Eleni's hands come
Everything changes.
First Istanbul steps out of the poem and takes its place
A child laughs
A tree opens into flower.

Before Eleni
When I was barely a child, before I'd got used to coffee and tobacco
Even before I knew mornings or nights
I once looked at night in my hands, in my eyes
Another time morning was all around me.

Eleni comes
I'm looking at the world
That day I realise the world's not as small as it's thought
We're not as unhappy in this world as we think
That day I said we should burn all poems and start again
A new *Brise Marine*
A new *Annabel Lee*.
It's with Eleni we realize
Why this sky rose up, why it came here
With her we understand why the sea packed up and went.

One day Eleni's hands come
For the first time the sea can be seen from a street.

II. YOUTH

My soul
Do you hear İlhan Berk crossing the bridge?
A sparrow is slowly flying by
A fish with its head through the water is looking around
A leaf is about to fall from the branch.

Lambodis took a bottle from the shelf and opened it.
A cloud stopped in the window
Lambodis went on with his job
Cleaned his hands, sliced cucumbers, tomatoes
Then sat and pondered his youth.

It was in a house
Eleni was eighteen, Ilyadis was twenty-three
Eleni knew songs
You couldn't imagine
        Coffeehouses all over Istanbul
        Pavement cafes indoor cafes
No matter how good the songs
They never could capture Eleni.

In those days Lambodis went everywhere in Istanbul with a cigarette
        in his mouth
Eleni's most beautiful features were her hands, her garlic
        smelling mouth
Lambodis wasn't yet a barkeeper
Lambodis wasn't yet anything
In those days they went every Sunday to Saint-Antoine
Eleni's breasts were peeled almonds
Her hands like pigeons
Even then Lambodis' enemies were many
The whole of Istanbul was behind Eleni.

Yes,
Lambodis' youth: a leaf about to fall.
He sat by the window, watched people come and go
Come look he said to me
Look, people are going by
I watch them when I'm bored
And forget all my troubles
We forget all our troubles.

My soul, it's always the same
A man a woman doing the same thing
Soon I'll get up and go to Sirkeci
My sweetheart's leaving on a train
One day the sun won't rise, there'll be no morning,
    we fear one day it will be as if we're not in the world.

This will all come to pass, my soul
One day we'll see Istanbul is beautiful
Thereafter Istanbul is always beautiful
A long long time ago the world was much more beautiful, for
    example
Those clouds this sky was a place we could reach out and touch
Now they only exist in poems
It all comes down to this, my soul

This world is beautiful
And Gülhane Park is full of trees.

III. SAINT-ANTOINE'S TIME OF LOVEMAKING

This sky
Is not like this everyday above Saint-Antoine
It's certainly time to make love
Windows are opened first
Ants crawl out of their nest
Mosses stir
Sky draws taut like a drum
A girl stitching in her window is happy for the first time
Homes and coffeehouses facing the sea are happy for the first time
For now Lambodis has nothing to fear
Eleni has nothing to fear
The pigeons will all take flight and no one will know fear
An hour when everything wakes
Love will begin
Everything will stop
A girl's hand stretching out to her dress will stop
Saint-Antoine will rise from his sarcophagus and walk off
        to a place on the coast
With him tombs and holy relics, Jesus himself
        will follow on behind
In everything's place there will be love
Chairs
Windows
Saint-Antoine's ceiling will walk straight to another ceiling
A door straight to another door
Nothing will want to be smaller
You'll see the sky grow large
The sea more blue
This love will go from eye to eye like a dark complexion
Going now to Istanbul along with all the best songs
Now, no matter where, a girls hand, her mouth, grow for this
For this a child clings to its mother's breast

Saint-Antoine's pigeons
Fly for this
The anxiety of order in poetry is for this
This sky can have no other meaning.

IV. Childhood in Fener

Saint-Antoine's childhood
Was spent in Fener

He's just started going to church
The first picture he sees is Jesus' lemon coloured face
The slender legs.
A cloud caught in the window
A child a little older than he is praying
The entire mass of saints suddenly pass before his eyes
The candle falls from his hand.
In those days Antoine's father was a shoemaker in Karaköy
He loved God as he loved his hammer and anvil
In those days it rained everyday in Istanbul

One day he stops in front of Hagia Dikolas' sarcophagus
Who knows how much the sea is missed, he thought
A window opens
They look at the sea
Then he goes home
And explains it all.

Childhood in fener:
First contact with the sea.

V. MORNING

Saint-Antoine recalls a morning
Like mornings which brought with them Ilyadis' songs.
One morning he gathers himself and enters the street
Gazing at shop windows, sky, cinema posters
I am with the new morning for the first time, he says to himself
The first time encountering sea
The first time with poetry.
That day, the whole day, he watches the street
He draws children indoors and talks about improbable things
There is no God, for example, he says
Later together they walk over the bridge
First he says hello to the sea
Then he returns to his place
He sees all the saints have awoken and washed their faces
There is something about this
Saints work like all of us
Some clean windows
Some carry water.

That day there is no evening
Morning never ends.

VI. ELENI LIGHT

One morning Saint-Antoine goes to Iaos Yokios
Night descends on the journey.
Suddenly he remembers Fotini Nermeroğlu
and goes to Fotini Nermeroğlu's house.
His Holiness Saint-Antoine is here, says Fotini
The whole of Zürefa Street proffers coffee from its windows
The girls hastily cover their breasts with their hands
Elpiniki gazes at the stars and everything's in its rightful place
Marvido Apiyos, Eftelya and Hagia Feya, Hagia Dikolas followed by
    Galata Tower, enormous Yüksekkaldirim and Eleni's mouth
    as beautiful as this world all follow on into Fotini's house.
Saint-Antoine looks at the world, "The world's not all that bad,
    Fotini Nermeroglu's not bad at all," he says to himself.
He asks for a Bible
They give him one.
He takes it, crosses out here and there, writes it anew.
Teo Fano, Maneli, Avi Antimos and Kalina step down off a cloud
Salome is on her knees
No, says Antoine at first, there are no longer such things, he says
He raises Salome to her feet
He holds out a Bible to Kalina
From now on, he says, this is the Bible.

Eleni's groin suddenly radiates light
The universe is suddenly sparkling.

VII. Sky

A cloud above Istanbul
White cloud yellow cloud black cloud

5 in the morning
not a sound in Saint-Antoine
what did he do, this man asks
then he answers himself
when we were all asleep
he stole the sky.
What can we do
but hang him.

Ha ha
Ha ha

What do the crowds have to say,
For three days we can't pray
There is no sky

My soul snapped the rope,
the sky is about to fall

What a strange thing this sky
like a handkerchief
we didn't think it would fit in a pocket.

The crowds stir
Who will pull the rope?
Someone says something
calls out

It's nothing

That day there is no evening
Morning never ends.

from Woodcuts

STEPPE

Get ready now
from here on not a single tree to be seen.

YESHILYURT STREET

This is all the street saw:
a man unloading a wagon
a passing child
a woman watching them both.

COUNTRY LIFE

A hair tent.
Three chickens.
All for a country life.

SUNSET

Sunset. Silently falls
below the plain.

—I drive birds into the sky.

SUN

Sun comes out, takes up its watercolour set.
Sits on the rooftop.

Repeats itself.

AUTUMN III

Autumn putting on its sock
—for a journey?

PICTURE

In dry grass
two horses graze,
a woman hangs laundry on a line.

Unknowingly, they magnify the plain.

WINDOW

A yellowed samovar
and a white handkerchief,

as though a window.

PLANE TREE LEAF

Who knows what this leaf of the plane tree inspires
in a poet with ten books to his name.

Forest

The forest quickly pulled in its fishing line
and said "Sun". He wrote the sun.

Empty sky. He loved the sky's emptiness.
A cormorant sang. The forest didn't care.

From a valley an old hornbeam laughed,
he thought the wind was passing by.

He left the beeches, shook their branches.
"It's rain" he said. Lightning struck the water.

That's when I knew I was in a forest.
Soldiers were going down the road, double file.

An Old Street in Pera

Birds take to the air above Hagia Irene
stalks of grass behind their ears.

At last you're here I say to myself
here where the roads of an old map meet.

A cat stares at you wide-eyed
and the sky is as low as it gets.

A woman is trying to cross the street. I think of you,
and say the neck I've never seen is terribly thin.

Peddlers, soldiers, knife grinders pass me by
and the sullen faced grave diggers of our world.

A voice says we're with you on the same peninsula,
then vanishes into an old Pera street.

So it is every night I tread an old street in Pera,
every night your mud on my soles.

Each Day I Walk from One End of a Market to the Other

It's my death, the thing you stand before
Its memory a washed out shore
Perhaps a tree-lined lane we once passed
(In the form of evening
                a time of love-making)
For tree-lined lanes do have a soul,
Whatever
        that is.

You are a rose,
                oh rose!
(So much, much more, so very much)
Each day I walk from one end of a market to the other
Looking at trees, pausing by a fountain
A bird draws up the whole street with its flight
—A little later your face
I think to myself
A woman's baroque laundry hangs on a line
Pours its brilliant white breath into my mouth
Later, you hold me delicately, kiss me
Once more I walk from one end of the market to the other.

from Delta and Child

PASSERBY

A swift, a puddle, a piece of sky.
They must have dropped from a poem.

So said the passerby.

SAGE

They left with sage in their mouths.
In those days man had the power to create silence.

Clocks

That day he left home, sat beside the sea,
and the shade read ten degrees late on the sundial.

Quinces

—Eat quinces!
God will even take note of that.

AUTUMN

March enters the plain, so it's autumn in the mountains!

BIRDS

Empty sky. Birds fly in from the right.

Forest

Somewhere, someplace, a forest has entered a poem.

Tobacco

When I wrote all this I was fifty-one
and my quilts smelled of tobacco.

Now as a Little Rose Goes Through the World

Wet your hair like that and ask night to comb it
Now as a little rose goes through the world
Let it tell of a shore-pounding death
Death which comes now, and then later
Death that dries wild flowers in notebooks
Death as a pale, silent easterner
Death that is a mountain or a river
Death that talks to itself as if talking to you
Death like death itself

Yes, wet your hair like that and ask night to comb it.

The Thames

I

Turner sketches the Thames. A northern tributary. Ash smelling.

Was Turner tall? He loved long rivers and the Thames.

Sky like mud.

And Death slowly stroles around as if laying eggs
waving to the Thames from a hill
(as if readying for winter
                          or for pain).

The Mersey and Humber rivers flow

slowly Thames keels are toyed

a clock strikes three at a crossroads

a cormorant flies in and flies off
a man is selling spermacetti candles
and sticking a stamp on his letter.

It's 1962, I'm in a house in Elsworthy working on a history of a river,
a river as thick as a grammar book and as old as a Genonese
    sledgehammer
in Galata.

At night I'm out to Piccadilly sitting on a stone
    flushing a pigeon into flight
I break a glass with a black man in a bar and stare
    long and hard at a woman, at a twisting road and
I take up the Thames and go, then perhaps it's another river, the
    Bosphorus
(so it's the Bosphorus and Asafpasha mansion, its divans and
    delicate curtains
a canary—from the Philipines, yellow, it never sings or else the
    canary I'm looking at
is a window—the interiors of dark rooms, lanterns, kitchen
    hands (mostly Armenian), the men's room, frying pans,
    plates, knifes and forks and lamps, fuses, maces, brazier
    coals, administrators, the little woman, a key, robes and
jackets,
Louis XIV broadcloth shawls and chairs
and a ferry with twin propellers, a round sternpost—and a
    French kitchen top
older than death
in the middle of July).

Perhaps too a fish, a sword fish—obstinate, dumb—and bluefish
    and mackerel
or else nothing at all.

But I keep a diary in a park and write B O R E D O M ten times in a
    notebook
(a book you bought one morning from Shishane hill from a man
    whose hands
spent hours crafting the book
his strange face
that now appears on the full page)
and I stare at a red carnation in the lapel of a passing
    Englishman
and geraniums.

Here the Thames is like the Danube
thin skinned
and like the timid Golden Horn on the Orthodox shore
and howls in the night in a language I've never heard
with its counter currents and darkness
like a white woman's waking face.

Suddenly I lose her trail at Abbey. She: the Thames. Maybe she's
    entered a lokanta.
Cooled some food. Looked out from a window. Listened to a
    kettle boiling on a stove. Watched its steam rising.
    Wondering why its water boils. And thought about the
    days of the week: Monday Tuesday Wednesday Thursday
    Friday Saturday Sunday. How bored God is on a Sunday.
    His wearing a cravat. How it rained so slowly that day.
    How the wind limped around. How the sun withdraws
    into its room. How she'd closed the curtains and read
    poems not wanting anyone to see. And then the sun's
    light.—Sunlight: *I'm here! I'm here!* It said—Perhaps she got
    lost with a boy from the palace, I say. She washed the
    threshold of a house. Or greeted T.S. Eliot in Trafalgar
    Square. And maybe flowed in and out of The Waste Lands.
    Studied physical education. Practised gymnastics.
    Stretched out her arms and legs. Considered her length.
    Found her width. Worked out the mean. Multiplied.
    Passed beyond her tributaries. Wrote that down too.
    Passed onward to Greenwich and Blackwall.

She sat down or thought first of the seas. Absorbed China. And
    Ceylan, Malta,
Jamaica, the Bahamas, Bermuda, Gabralta, Canada.

Later Australia, New Zealand, India and Africa and the crown
    republics (*reminders of*
botanic exiles—H.G. Wells) and the British Navy and the Ancient
    History of the Assyrians and a fur trade centre, Hudson
    Bay Company and other companies, rail networks and
    steam ships and two places of exile and a bundle of
    possessions and Defoe and Fielding's satires.

And then our own: Namik Kemal riding a horse to the theatre,
    Sultan Aziz and his
garter and Ziya Pasha, behind them prisoners doing hard labour
    and women and men's hats and slavery and bulls and
    horses and The History of Work and John Locke, Jesus of
    Nazareth & the saying: *itiseasierforacameltopassthrough*
    theeyeofaneedlethanforarichmantoenterthekingdomofheaven! And
    the 1st and 2nd International and a muddy-footed-giant
    (by the name of Imperialism) and her own dirty history

Edwards the I, II and III

The Commonwealth and male sex organs

                        (the first birds with mammals)

Then she strips off as in the days of Rome. Hangs up her robes.
    My 160 miles! She says. Looks at a picture on the wall. Her
    own picture. A river like a snake. And twisted. Curling
    upward towards the city. Going down at Limehouse. To the
    West Indies. And stops to look at herself passing St. Paul's
    Cathedral. Coming as far as Bow Church. Then stretching
    out around St. Dunston. Crossing over

                            (and)

Stroles around at Customs House. Spins a barrel with a
     fisherman. They go in and out
of houses. She seizes hold of a crucifix, a window. They head
     towards Oxford Street (you know Oxford Street). She
     bought a banana. Drank a bottle of milk. And said: *It's
     evening!* And as she stopped two swallows passed each
     other in flight. First she sent a man on his way to St. Paul's
     (*I need to go to Hungry. You should ready yourself, I'm passing
     the Danube!*) At Hyde Park paper fell from her pockets. And
     there she sat with a Scot.

Then she strikes Blackfriars Bridge and goes on to Bankside.

Crisscrosses up a small rise and gains the centre with a
     fisherman
passes through stations, winches, the smell of leather. Throws
     out her fishing line
and she comes to a stop beside a piece of Staffordshire porcelain.

II

Is this the morning of 1962? Overcast. Foggy.
A face like Queen Victoria—always gazing off at a distance
and always using her left hand
she never placed her hands on chairs
which is why she always woke at night and changed the water
    of her geraniums
and hash plant—

and morning, always that morning on the road to Hanley. Hasty
with small feet
but St. George is peevish and at Rotten Row
she enters a church without taking off her shoes. And never sits

and is jealous of Jesus.

And June is about to fall on the river
and sweet chestnut trees

and a child spins a wheel in a shop and says I haven't slept since
last night

and a girl sizes up dantella and tülle to a curtain edge. Her face
like paper.

And a man is kneeding dough in a bakery and can only read the
Manifesto in dialect

and there is a watch with a flywheel in the shape of a question
mark near Hardwich

and the sun is shown with a giant U and the water is 4 + 4

and the watermill on the banks of the Mosel River is as it was in the
time of the great Karl
a fountain pen
and cotton paper still comes from China to Middle Gardner Street
and to Temple
and to Dombart
Roundtown takes a right at Dombart, takes the night and wash-
ing on a line.

At St. Petrus again I lose and then refind the Thames.
And every morning God appears in the form of a glass of water
dresses and goes out into Elsworthy Street looking for a friend
and takes a magnetic needle from the Arabs and gives it to the
          Europeans in 1180
and eyeglasses to Florenza
and uses bonds
lights up London Street in the XV century
makes pocketwatches tick and birds eat grapes
Is carbon an acid? She later asks. If not it's eternal, she says.
Then lifts the lid on Nature's Dialectics
proclaims the immortality of Protein
and turns her head towards the Thames
(Thames: *Where am I?* She thinks)
counting the bridges to herself
moves off towards Greenwich. Sets her watch.
Is detained at Blackwall, seeks out docks, enters and comes out
          of a canal
crosses to a small island, lingers around houses
(and again thinks of Australia, India, Africa, islands, the
          Carribean, Cretean
                    oils, broad beans, dill,
                              and finally comes right to now)

God is in the service of the English! She says. And lays down.

And the wind's arm falls.

You

I looked you over. Your voice, old and alone
I undressed you. Your plentiful mouth.

I take in your eyes. Your eyes
are the Middle Ages. Vast and uninhabited.

I take hold of your hands and say white,
your pale white naked flesh, your loins.

I part your loins. Your scent
is the scent of sky and of trees.

I lay down and claim your voice
your voice! Istanbul. Elgin. Eternal.

We emerge onto a steep rampart. I dismount
from my horse. I'm white. You're white.

Epilogue

Later I spent the whole day stroling around
I wrote this poem, maybe you heard.

I Woke Saying I Love You Three Times

I woke saying I love you three times
I got up and changed the water in the vase
I saw a cloud had just upped sticks and left.

Your face was fallen as if from some part of the morning.

I kicked out a poem with half-finished streets and balconies
Got bored, made food, dried myself some herbs
My cherry laurel! I heard a voice say.

Your face was like the first days of the Republic.

I went out and walked around up and down
I read some poems and formed an affinity
I felt your clove-gum smelling breath on me.

I wear you out remembering but still you're beautiful.

Thank You

Yes, it was for your mouth, always open, moving;
For this, the fractious blue of the sky;
For the apple scented Turkish you spoke
For this miserable, worthless memory of death
For the streets that everyday become a markteplace
For your voice like children returning from school

For all this, for all of these, I thank you.

Istanbul

A small, flat rectangle. And a heading: *Istanbul, 1574; Braun-Hogenberger. Gravuré.*

A subscript. Below the picture, centred in Gothic lettering: BYZANTYUM LUNC CONSTANTINOPOLIS (or so I read it). Clearly from Hogenberger's own hand. Piece by piece he begins to weave the picture: sets down lines, triangles, rectangles. Ups perpendiculars. Attractive. Autonomous. Establishing Hogenberger's own alphabet, tranformed into the great vocabulary of ISTANBUL. On wood. A gravure, then, to be scoured out with a steel pen. Repeatedly looking at the lithograph. Given by a Galata Jew. He sensed the soul of a Bohemian engraver in Hogenberger *(longtime seller of mulberries and figs. A bit of a mapmaker too, as a man who had travelled around. He lives at the Guild. These days he works on wood. At night he spreads before him pictures of Istanbul. The seven hills. The plains. The valleys. The reinforced walls. As in this engraving. This engraving: isn't this the point I want to come to? Could this prologue have any other meaning? Like all prologues it is an addition and unneccessary. But impossible without it. Think of all those masters! Which has saved himself from them? And entered straight upon the subject? Like those beautiful textbooks. Simple and direct. A table of contents on the first page, in bold print, geometrically placed one below the other. Which is fine, but why don't we come straight to the point? Without longwinded words. And with a rough outline of the subject. And without delving into history? For instance, to say it's a peninsula).*

A peninsula. Imitating a triangle. Three-dimensional. Horizontal and distended. Rising to a peak. And drawing a line at the Golden Horn. And descending to bays and islands. To a continent. From three sides and up above. Because this is a bird's eye view.—*And it shall remain so.* Completing itself with a straight 18 miles. With its inlets and promontories. It will close in and straighten its peaks. From seven points, silent and steep. Entering roads and streets. Crossing a long, narrow strait. To die in a sea commemorated in Greek letters. With a margianl note: TÜRKELI. Three seas (it's always how maps of Istanbul are seen, from a bird's eye view). And there it rests in bays with its S's and U shapes. Then returns again to itself. Again leaving islands—like outstretched feet. Throwing out arms like an octopus. To reproduce there, separate from its body. And old men: in the courtyards of mosques, holding childrens' hands. Sleeping with children, their beautiful mouths. And dark. And Imperial (that's how Hogenberger approached it too: dark and full of sorrow). That's why he engraves using black dyes, black ink. On wood. Veinless. Smooth. Drying in the sun. The grease still seeps out. And now it is slippery under his hand. Walnut. Different from itself. Because that's how it has always lived. Those migrants, those fires, have served no other use than to augment its loneliness. That's why it's Türkeli, the land of the Turks. Straight and calm. And still like that. Those ramparts were not built for nothing: two floors high and steep. For all of this, lonely and by itself. Right-facing, protruding. As far as they can be on this engraving. Indistinct. Since the city appears on paper it will leave its name, and that of Hogenberger, to history. Even if Pera and Galata slowly become transparent. With its 12 gates. Its tower of Christ. And its Latin inscriptions. Since he's making a picture he should use shadows. Dark, light, even lighter. Always taking notes. Measuring proportions like all mapmakers. It's a picture-map he makes. Isn't it clear from the roads' contours? With their black, curved lines. The sea left white. And the Bosphorus. A peninsula then.

That's why he scours. The thought of a picture: for a monograph. Contemporary. He has thought of our times. Peppered his engraving with portraits of the sultans: Orhan, Murat I, Beyazit I, Mehmet I, Murat II, Selim the Grim, Beyazit II. With Mehmet the Conquerer in the centre. Long-faced and bearded. Larger than all the rest. Only Süleyman the Magnificent on horseback. Dark, with large eyes. (*You know Süleyman the Magnificent: wide-browed and short-legged. Unsmiling. That's why he never used concubines. He used face-powder and mascara.*) Three horsemen clear the way. Armed. They look ahead. And obstruct the front of Tophane, in a circle. Full face and in profile. In quilled and crested turbans. Past Venetian made galleys (*is he not Venetian himself? Of German origin. From Aksoy. He never leaves Galata. For that is where he is looking from. The sun on his back, pencil in hand*). Now we see the Imperial mosques one by one. All speaking the same language. An agile tongue. Extending in width towards the top. Like a well-finished quatrain. Only the houses rise and the waterside residences descend. And they do. Always with a steel pencil, scratching his signature. Now he returns to Langa. He longs for the sea. But first he stops at Karaköy. Now he engraves childrens voices. Carves out a bird. Lifts out a fish etc. It's the turn of Istanbul grasses now. He works in a leaf, then a cypress, as an old inhabitant of Üsküdar. He raises up a tombstone. Draws Balkapan Inn with a thick line, so it stays within its frame. But it doesn't. He wanders off to Seven Hills.

He rubs past the Tower of Almenas. Leaves the Ramparts of Theodosia on the right. Now he rests beside a cross. In his hand a yellowed figure of Jesus. He kisses it. And again he engraves battle walls and summer palaces. He stops in front of a waterside house. With two doors. Dark. To have a better look at Seraglio Point and at Topkapi. A city. 699,000^{m2}. A ceiling: domed, in mother-of-pearl. A long eulogy. Guards. Thick, stone walls. Four rectangles. One inside the other. As if a rising Tower of Babel. Wooded. Tasselled guards: colliding with a galley. Finally into the Hippodrome. A pentagonal shape, head in hand with John the Evangelist. To gaze at the palace birds? Or the Egyptian obelisk? With its copper sphere. Noted in Neshri's history. Now he will look out of a coffehouse window. His cross dangling. His eyes fixed on Süleymaniye mosque. Its great courtyard. And four corners. And there he lingers, drinking tea. Melling's engraving in his hand (*or is that what I say, thinking of Melling. Dear Melling! And Selim III, who never could leave birdshops and spice-shops alone. Wearing a stambouline*). Now where is he? At Yüksekkaldirim? Hagia Nicolas? The Thousand-and-one columns? (or else). He turns his face to Hagia Sophia. Bolt upright. A straight line. It breaks at Petrios Gate. Into the shape of a *tughra*, an Ottoman seal. After a while he will go down to the coast, reading a map by Piri Reis, stopping often on his way.

According to Asagik and Lazarus, an island. Full of ins and outs, and Armenians. With inner fortifications 20 feet thick. Outer walls of 10 feet. 225 turrets. Caucasian horsemen. Andreas, first bishop. John, a saint. Stakis, who wrote him a greeting. Macedonius, first consul. Photius, the last patriarch. Hagia Irene, a church (not seen). John, a baptist and gout-ridden like Mehmet the Conquerer. Rosario, a virgin. Michael, emperor. Hydraulis, an aqueduct. Khrisi Pili, a building. Hovannesian, a moneylender (*from Pera. Sleeps in his shop. A follower of Lazarus. And, like Ahmet I, he hates the number 14*). Ayvansaray's suburbs with its 17 Jewish districts. Gothic columns. Obelisks. Horses and donkeys. And Inns. This is why it's an island. But it will also be an engraving. On wood. It tangles around houses, walls, books, strikes metals, iron, zinc, goes out with women. But will always remain on wood. To die there. Always to be Istanbul. Around 1574. Or a morning? And today. This hour. Unchanged. In its law of motionlessness. Then it will return to its wall. Its origin, an engraving. With its Theodosian moats. As it is:
    Berk-like. And

he stops. Because he's at Galata. A district. With two steep slopes. With ditches and curves. They're filling in the sea. An Arab blocks his view. Night is announced in Latin. Chains are drawn. And its 12 gates. Its bitter waters. 146 steps. Its sleepless monasteries. And Voyvodas. Its squares. Its Latin church. The embossed silver icon of Mary, made by Lucas. Sent to Pulcheria by Theodosus the Younger's wife Eudoxia, which Pulcheria always carried by her side. Mary, who appeared to two blind men at Hagia Dicolas where they regained their sight but never saw her again. Surrounded by battlements. Venetian and Pisan. Where the bowmen were placed. There, to live in the towers 47 years, 13 days and 5 hours.

But let us again return to the engraving. And to Hogenberger. And let's describe whatever we see. In the first person. And the present tense. The closest and quickest path to reality (because it starts with I see). Therefore: O my eyes! You should start because I see a road, far off. Winding towards Psamathia along the city-wall. Aren't there a lot of walls? You say. Could it be any other way? Now that it's the entrance to a road, it must be closed. By wind. Medieval. So, what else do you see? Hills? Cut out by sky. It's true, we'd forgotten the sky. Like on a pirates map, one that never leaves Istanbul. Yes, that sky you see. With its Byzantine face. Was seen by Constantine the Great (*they say he was blonde. And very frightened. Because he had lived long. He wore scarlet robes, feared the Goths, loved the Visigoths. Bronze. Wood and stone*). And stop. Taking this engraving in your hand. Torn from a book and spread on the poet's table. He keeps looking at it, lighting his pipe. Every morning. In AtaCity (a terrible sentence but I won't cross it out). As he dresses. For a life: a place in which to wander, with Crusaders. A life, then. So let's stop. And end this. With parentheses—it's better this way. Wasn't this how we began? Then we should continue thus. With a parallel to the prologue. Without summary. Without annotation. Without "O"s—wringing the neck of poeticism. So there you are.

This Caesar weighed the land.

Denizens of Hristaki Arcade

I don't love evenings anymore, said Diran, there was a time when I loved evenings so much.

I don't want to remember anything. Why remember?

Everything's changed and left its place to a huge silence.

Mari still hasn't come back, said Ifijeni. Paluka must have shut up shop ages ago.

Why is it this Alba's breasts are so big, said Vartuhi, she's not even fourteen.

She's like her mother, said Marta, there was a time her breasts had no equal in Pera.

How many times did I tell you to have Izidor cut your hair, said Armenak, it's driving me mad.

Everything of yours gets on my nerves, everything.

How crowded Papillon's tat shop is, said Glavani, it's impossible to understand these women.

Memories make me fat like this, said Diran, from now on I don't want to touch another thing.

It's enough for me to look out of the window. See, Eleni is coming back, a blue bag in her hand.

She always wears high heeled shoes, always goes out alone.

Pigmalion has changed its display again, said Sara, stores don't know what to do.

What's your problem, said Marta, all day you jabber on like that.

So what? Don't you hear them every night making love upstairs, that's what I'm on about, said Sara.

Then they drink Chinese tea till evening and sit staring at the sky, I just don't get it.

The sky is ribbons, rag dolls, picture books, oranges from China.

This Luisa is now in her sixties, said Diran, and she still can't tear her head from the window.

Every night Lebon, Alkazar, Degustasion! She never gets enough of the world.

Every night, every night it's Hafiz Burhan, Osman Nihat, Hafiz Cemal on the old 78's.

Lulu's become very forgetful, said Germaine, she keeps asking how much water to put with the rice.

Yesterday she left the house to go to Shütte and found herself in Saint Terre church.

We've grown old, old, I can't even pick up two logs of wood from here to throw on the stove.

How many times have I told Yanni to bring me dry wood, he doesn't understand.

My side's been burning for a while, I'm shaking, said Eleni, and the doctor says I've nothing.

But I should sleep early, get up early, avoid getting cold, look after my health.

I also said that some mornings I wake up as a butterfly; these things happen.

So Sara has closed her windows, said Marta, she could never stop thinking about her husband who went away to sea on a banana boat.

Look how long Miss Suzan's neck is, Said Lulu, who does she look like?

There was a time when she couldn't care less, she wore yellow socks and bedded whoever she pleased.

Ulla is shouting again from the third floor that she's going to Markiz, said Diran.

Is she going to Markiz, said Madam Tilla, I hate the smell of resin, never liked it.

I saw Doctor Violi yesterday, said Eleni, when I was coming back from the Royal Hotel; he didn't recognize me.

He used to wave to me from Marta's window; how I used to laugh.

His house smelt always of carnations and oil; I came and went through the smell of carnations and oil.

For months, said Armenak, I've no desire to go to Nektar, right under my nose; what happened to me?

Beyoğlu is like a shroud now, no, a vinegar!

See, it's night, said Diran, we should close the windows, night has come.

Night, now, everything is night, for one or two hundred years, everything is night.

The world is full of loneliness, said Lulu, one minute I'm watering geraniums, the next I'm changing my clothes.

Ah, it never ends, said Armenak, that damned noise from downstairs, these sounds of drums and flutes.

I can't sleep looking at Margarita's hat and umbrella, said Marko.

How beautifully she used to sing those Tuscany ballads sitting right in front of me.

Now Time doesn't know how to pass: children, trees, the water-dead in water.

The smell of Matilda's skin, said Vartuhi, more than anything I can't forget that smell.

Her silk stockings, and her long legs, and her sleeping all night with a rose in her mouth.

And now at four o'clock I'm tossing and turning in my bed, tossing and turning.

This world's strangling me, this house, this window, these curtains, this toothbrush.

This is Madam Anahit's accordion, said Matilda, I grew up with this accordion.

Now she's playing those beautiful comparsitas and tangos to this dirty crowd.

Ah, I can't listen anymore to her butcher's songs, her onion smelling accordion.

This city, these walls, these radio noises are driving me crazy.

You're so right, said Suzan, I don't want to see this Long Road, these trees, these people anymore.

ALL TOGETHER

Forgive us, forgive us all you houses, streets, people, forgive us.

Forgive us old age, forgive us.

I Don't Want to Think

Nothing's as old as this world. The sky is sick. The sun is ordinary. The trees are unskilled. Every morning a Bedu goes to work on his camel. Every evening two Chinese walk their bird.

The world is a repetition. A tree looks a thousand years into the future. Sees a dinosaur a thousand years away. Ghazali used to liken himself to the number 7. Homer used to walk every morning.

There is nothing new to the eye.

This is terrifying.

Was it Göethe who said "Time is my field"? I don't want to know. From where it sits a house overlooks Montevideo. The chair is urban. The window is feudal. Water ran without memory. The soul is alone. When I was a child I wanted to be a river. Rivers always called to me. I don't want to think. The world thinks for me instead.

The word is dead.

Bronze: Monarchic.

Iron: Democratic.

One evening I suddenly saw that the world had grown old. Seeing wore me out.

Askelopis

Askelopis used to walk around with a bird from Ephesus and could see what we couldn't. Objects are like that; not everyone can see them. They love secrecy. Like poets, they too speak in a white language. Reason cannot grasp it. Yet there is nothing that is invisible. Objects don't know this. Why should they? After all, it's not for objects to know. Do fish know the water in which they swim? I recognized the forest without knowing it, and never forgot it*. There's no way of stopping them, once objects turn into words. They envelope the world, then turn into thousands of sentences. In some corner of the world, every morning, a thousand objects wake for this. I came to know the world through sentences. The outer limits of the universe. Language is the only god, that fetus!

(My beloved language, do not conceal those untrodden paths and keep me from seeing them.)

There's nothing more to objects than this. This much Askelopis could not see. Death revealed this to him. (Doesn't philosophy, after all, teach us something about death?)

Would you say objects are lonely?

From now on objects will never feel this kind of loneliness again.

I promise.

* O memory, there's no escaping you!

Rocks

ROCKS I

They're talking   about rocks
    I was a rock

        I heard them

ROCKS II

I grew
       in rock
      reach out

         to me

ROCKS III

A rock

        and a hill
are talking about death

    watching water

ROCKS IV

Hey

    rocks

       I'm evenings'
         spirit

A Turtledove Valantin Taskin

Valantin Taskin was born in a stately home in Caucasia in 1902.

He played with dolls to the age of three and with his beloved father's beard.

By the age of six he knew every bird by sound and name.

At seven he started piano lessons. The world was his.

At ten he played Chopin in front of the Char family.

He learned languages. "However many languages there are, that's how many worlds there are" his father had said. He never forgot it.

At seventeen picture books, maps of the world were forever in his hands.

He always likened himself to Sleeping Beauty.

At eighteen he married Constantin von Clodt Jurgenzburg. He separated one year later.

At twenty he developed a passion for insects. He found beauty in all that insects did.

He started a stamp collection. He believed he had come into the world in the form of a turtledove.

A diamond brooch and a pair of golden earrings were all he saved from the revolution. He cried his heart out in Istanbul.

Then suddenly he remembered he could play the piano. He accompanied the orchestra of La Bohéme at the Lüx Hayat hotel.

He played the mazurka in Tavernas. And met Todori.

For forty years now Todori sings while he plays.

Now in every photograph he's staring off into the distance, suddenly jolted by the way he's lived his life.

Letters and Sounds

Shihabüddin Fazullah spoke with thirty two letters and did not have a soul. He believed in letters and earned a living knitting skull caps. It is said he saw every letter in the human face. In the Zeyl he wrote to Cavidan (which hasn't been found), he assigned the letter A to sky; to water: C (water is from Thales); to death: U (Death is a bit U). To fire: Z.

The world was the letter, all forms. Sophocles, who like Pythagoras, did not know how to draw, was also of the letter, as was the cricket, and Mohammed too.

Mohammed (whom we know, spoke with twenty eight letters and had a soul and no bird could ever have flown to where he did) gave ear to sounds. He listened only to them. Everything was sound. Heaven and Hell were sound. A peacock was sound. If Tu Fu rode to Rice Pudding Mountain to graze his horse, it was sound. Which is why he always felt a void between the soul and the forms. And why he seldom wrote. Why should he? Language is lonely. It doesn't speak. The universe is more talkative than us, he said. More leaf-filled. The sun speaks with images. A tree works noisily. So does a stone. Night descends in noise. The universe is sound.

"The alphabet is a peddler."

Nevizade Street Greengrocer Ahmet Aslanoğlu

Thirty-five years Ahmet Aslanoğlu opened and closed Nevizade
    Street.
He loved green and knew no other colour but green.

For a long part of his childhood he observed the flight of birds.
He didn't understand birds at all.

In his old age (has it come to that already?)
The wine's bitter taste changed nothing.

When his work went well—for whatever reason—
He believed that God had suddenly sat on the sky.

Evenings he saw Orhan and Sait leaving Lambo
As they passed he always raised a smile behind their backs.

For thirty-five years Ahmet Aslanoğlu was a greengrocer
For thirty-five years he painted Nevizade Street green.

Whichever Angle We Take, Everything Explains Itself

Everything, everything began in the moon-watching city of Babel.

Names followed. Once named, everything became boring. The silence was broken. The enormous silence.

In history there are no animal names to be found, you say*. Nor the sounds of flowers' names . . . yet sound . . . is everywhere.

I don't forget that everything had it's place in the world. I saw that Time became unrecognizable once it acquired a name. A bird couldn't remember its name any-old-how. As for the mountains, not one of them knew its name.

Wonderful.

To name something is death!

Whichever angle we take, everything explains itself.

Memhet the Conqueror was short.

Amos was a farmer of Pharaoh figs.

Al Farabi was swarthy.

If only we'd never known names. The world we see through names is not the world. That's why we go to our graves never having seen the earth. There's nothing without its own weight. We should have started from here. Mad Time was left outside. We were separated. Now whatever we write we write about death; death and time.

* History, this phallus memory.

I don't know why but these days I read death vertically. Try it yourself. It's worth it.

I'm cutting it here. I hear a blade of grass talking as it does. I'll also be at the bird's birthday party. Night awaits me. We know the way.

Paris

The Seine divides Paris, pouring nowhere and to no death

Gare de l'Est, long like a winter's day and smelling of trees,
Shabby as a pilchard and full of noise

A man brushes his moustaches. He's as yellow as a Chinaman

A beech tree is writing silence and February in *Hausmann*

The Cardinal coffeehouse smells of wild thyme and old inlay
And bankers (did bankers wash corpses years ago and still weep
for it?)

Gramont Street is in the hand of the wind
Clearly it wants to be with God to sit in cafés, take morning strolls
Then takes stamps from the hands of an aged philatelist
To cross the Seine, go to *Saint-Germain* and sit in Lipp's
Then draw pictures on pavements, dance to a kasap air

And then return

Does this street lead to Montparnasse? Or to a shop selling wild
    herbs and silent
voiceless flowers
And a denizen of the Red Sea who slept with a woman -
    someone muttering,
wandering through the streets of Alexandria,
Who woke startled one morning in autumn in a small
    coffeehouse, next to him a bottle of olive oil and
    loneliness. Boulevard Hausmann stretches far away and a
    man,
The Song of Maldoror under his arm
and de Sade. Wizen-faced like an Eskimo, walking alone, waking
    alone on the hotel's
fifth floor.
Brews tea. One who listens to the life of creaking wood
Wanders always underground
and does not wash

So there it is about to turn past *Notre-Dame* and the night

And the Île-Saint-Louis (or a white house: "playing old
    Macedonian thieves songs
that start out with the line—*If only I were in your bed now!*

And fixing his eyes on Crete, as if photographing the sun,

And copying monastic rules at night and wandering with a
    forest in his pocket").

The Seine thins out at Saint-Michel. And beds down
At Charanton like a shy student in his dorm

At the Pont de Sevres like a bandit's den

As young as paper announcing births

And filthy mid July

Stroking pre-pubescent moustaches, and the dark rue *Condé*

Leads to the Odéon and is as lonely as a breadcrumb

Two women pass by and they have never heard of the Marquis
de Sade
And azaleas

An Austrian girl's face is listening to Bach
And so are the slender hands of a poet

And a boy goes past carrying a freshwater fish he's caught

Rue Danton is like a brushed tooth

And your face
Your face like a pen found on the coast
Like an unending gulf-stream undertow
And with that rugged
Face of yours I climb *Sacré-Coeur*

Your hands grow small, you don't know where to put them
And your voluminous mouth, except on the whitest of days

Is this rue Cujas? Where you strolled with an Algerian who kept
his money
in a pouch,
Carried a knife, had an amber cigarette-holder and a face the
size of a hand

In Cluny you look at a Book of Hours (A man is picking wheat/ a
    thin stream flows
under a thin bridge/ A woman's mouth waves goodbye from her
    chateau/ A stopped water clock/ And I climb a hideously
    long road)

A student charms a snake in the Place de l'Étoile
His face like a painting
He blows his nose loudly as I pass, bends and pulls up his boots

Paris is like a box. The inclined head of a violin. To the left, yet
    again, the Louvre and Charles V. The Bastille? The Bastille
    is unseen. So—Louis XIV has not yet said, 'I am the law!'
    And Charles V hasn't yet grown a moustache. *And yellow
    dye had not been found. Organs were played with water. The post
    horse is about to come in, so too the fob watch and fireworks, the
    musket and the pedal piano. And the temperature scale. But the
    rectangle was already known.* The Tuilleries like the Louvre's
    right arm. And this leads to a square by Saint-Honoré. And
    there's no one there. Hubert Robert's wife is waiting for
    the street lamps. Half of Saint-Germain is visible. A street
    crosses Richlieu. A man gets into a carriage. The Place de
    Carousel is long and never sees the Seine. They work with
    ropes as in the time of Louis XV. Will we wait for
    Louis XV's time to see the sky and Pont-Neuf? And salted
    herrings (herrings were salted in the Thirteenth Century—
    Engels), Sainte-Chapelle, l'Arbre de Mai and the Tour de
    l'Horloge. Earth hollowed, chasmed, canyoned. A destitute
    woman gouging holes in a doorpost. And Voltaire's face.
    (I'm in rue Nazarin. In a small restaurant with a black
    man. He stares constantly ahead of himself. Perhaps he's
    thinking of a poem which has two meanings in Chinese.
    Or else he's undressing a woman on the third floor of a
    hotel, a woman who always lived alone, who writes the

word 'winter' in an ancient script, whose hands assume a
pose no longer used. With short eyelashes, a moustache
and a signet ring. She's probably turning into Solforino
now. Buying kerosene as she passes the oil yard, the
ironworks, the carpenters, the flint-makers. And she peels
off her clothes, crushes garlic, mixes it with herbs

and sees me for the first time)

Is this crowd welcoming Henri II? Or does it welcome rain
        always slanting
through a poem?

The sun moved to the right side of the Eiffel Tower. Put on its
        corpse. Withdrew

The Île-Saint-Louis, like a glass of water,

As if revealing the wide arc of death

Like the coping stone of a building

Suddenly I take your mouth into mine like a desolate rose
It is as if mounting a white horse
We gallop past trees timber bridges

Saint-Denis is like thuluth script

I breathe in lungfuls of frankincense in a Greek church

Your face is waxy. I am thinking of a rhyme for your face

Sainte-Clotilde stands motionless

And I think the Eiffel Tower is the longest of shadows
And the Pont de Sully

Franco, assassin! A man writes in chalk on a wall
And a crucifix falls upon the day

The bells of Sainte-Clotilde ring out unceasingly

My bed is cold. I work on a poem *Season of the Hunt*. And I say to
    myself one day
I must write the rooftops of Paris
And then its sky

The sky over Saint-Jacques is like an unfamiliar poem
And at Versailles and Chartres it never was

Noises coming from Les Invalides. And a bird is weaving silence
    into the air
I say again, I must write these Paris rooftops.
Then the fruit market. Sundays in Paris. Its butcher's wives. Of
    Cihat
Burak. Of Güzin's face
And its city walls.

Saying all this I duck into a street
Paris is like a fleet of steamships
And sadness is the best rhyme I've found

Evening arrived over Pigalle in Sunday clothes. Went in and out
    of shops.

Wandered around in rue Cauchois. Wore pink shirts. Stretched
    out.

Now we wander the streets together. The fourth floor of a house.
In a room.

A mason and I hold a plumb line in Concorde

The sky is about to fall in Monmartre

We call in on a student who writes one of Nâzım's poems in a
    notebook

We bandage an injured worker. Together we close and open a
    shop.

A bas toutes les dictatures! a girl screams out

And the wind gathers up the leaves in the Luxembourg Park
And Paris is like a striker's face near the Sorbonne

And children children children the sky falling

Poet and Voices

Everyday he comes and takes his place in the world.
"The difficult thing," he says "is to live the life of poetry,
writing always comes later." The words come easy
from his mouth, like ordering a glass of water.
Then, to be more at home with himself
he goes as usual to his old chair and sits.
Comes face to face with trees, with seas and skies.
He twirls a carnation in his hands. Brings it to his nose.
Then listens to the voices. To someone saying goodnight,
someone passing in the street. Mornings' noisy departure.
Silent grass. Descending day.
                    Voices. Voices. Voices.
All day he listens to these sounds
and then withdraws
                    to his place in the world.

Afterword

from The Secret History of Poetry

"In the Tang dynasty civil servants were chosen
for their knowledge of poetry."

Poets are island dwellers . . .

～

All poets are in the service of masters. Just as all shoeshines work for the best . . .

～

The difficult thing is to live the life of poetry; writing always comes later.

～

Poetry is a fetus.

～

It's an image thing. With the poet it comes into existence. That's why every poet has their own way of using image, an image-key: a key that allows him to open and close the lock of his own devising.

～

If a poem is written and goes out into the world, something in the world has changed.

～

Poetry is contrary to all forms of correctness, even itself.

～

Poetry is spontaneous. A sea, a tree, a face, a street that's suddenly there.

~

Poetry is wild. It's where the kick comes from.

~

Poetry is a hidden spring. It cannot be opened or explained; the thing it wants to explain, to show, is itself.

~

It's the job of poetry to light fires.

~

Poets are children. I don't mean they don't grow up. They do, but always as children grow. The oldest they reach is adolescence.

~

The language of poetry is a language used nowhere else.

~

Poetry is on paper.

Mostly it's a single page. That's where it gives colour, where it's born and lives . . .

That's why, as soon as the poem begins to take form in the poet's mind, he sees the page.

~

Poetry is interrogation.

~

Residues:

1.
The coffin was opened and the waking face seen.

2.
Her voice was like the flight of a child's kite.

3.
The long wishing-thread was never broken.

4.
Time came when the horse became its own saddle.

~

To whoever and whenever poems come they pull you to one side. From that point on the sky is no longer the sky.

~

Poets carry people, cities, rivers and streets in their pockets.

~

The poet destoys to rebuild . . .

～

What poetry writes is silence. A silence like the stopping of the world, the severing of its breath.

～

Faultless, perfect poems are not easy to write. But the truely difficult thing is to write easy, flawed poems.

～

Shelley was infatuated with the image-power of Bacon's essays. He looked at them with the eyes of a poet. It needn't surprise us. For the same reason I too look at a lot of prose with a poet's eye. And a lot of poems from the point of view of prose.

The sole key that opens and closes the poem is image.

～

Poets write in parentheses . . .

Printed in the United States
78402LV00002B/80

9 781844 712748